This book belongs to

- -

Big Handwriting Practice Workbook for Kids

13-Digit ISBN: 978-1-40035-301-9
10-Digit ISBN: 1-40035-301-7

Books published by Cider Mill Press Book Publishers are available at special discounts for bulk purchases in the United States by corporations, institutions, and other organizations. For more information, please contact the publisher.

Applesauce Press is an imprint of
Cider Mill Press Book Publishers
"Where good books are ready for press"
501 Nelson Place
Nashville, Tennessee 37214, USA

cidermillpress.com

HarperCollins Publishers, Macken House, 39/40 Mayor Street Upper,
Dublin 1, D01 C9W8, Ireland (https://www.harpercollins.com)

Typography: Report, Scandia, Sofia Pro
Image Credits: Illustrations used under official license from Shutterstock.com.

Printed in Canada
25 26 27 28 29 TC 5 4 3 2 1
First Edition

BIG
Handwriting
Practice
Workbook
FOR KIDS

Pen Control, Letter Tracing,
Writing Activities, and More!

Crystal Radke

APPLESAUCE PRESS

Dear Parents, Caregivers, and Educators,

Welcome to an exciting learning journey with *Big Handwriting Practice Workbook for Kids*! This book will help young learners develop essential early writing skills as well as a love for learning through fun, engaging, and educational activities.

Help your child get the most out of this workbook with these tips:

Fine Motor Skills Exercises: Activities like cutting, coloring, threading beads, and playing with small objects will help your child develop a strong tripod grasp, which is essential for proper handwriting. Encourage your child to exercise their skills daily with these toys and games.

Proper Tools: Small hands and muscles need small tools. Providing your child with crayons, small pencils, or short markers will help them develop the proper tripod grasp and strengthen their hand muscles.

Proper Workspace: A well-lit area with a child-sized table and chair will help your little writer focus. Make sure the book is placed on a hard surface for writing.

Learning Pace: Follow your child's pace. Every child learns and grows at their own speed, so allow your child to lead the way. Keep sessions short and playful to maintain enthusiasm. No matter the pace, encourage your child with positive reinforcement as they practice to help build confidence.

Practice: A few minutes of writing daily will build muscle memory and confidence over time.

Model and Engage: Writing together can be a great bonding experience. Try sky writing, tracing letters in shaving cream or sand, and playing "my turn, your turn" activities to make learning interactive and fun.

With patience, encouragement, and consistent practice, your little one will be on the path to handwriting success!

Pre-Writing and Pen Control

Before your child begins writing on paper, it's vital to strengthen their fine motor skills and hand–eye coordination through fun, hands-on activities off the page. The five exercises below will help your child build the muscle strength needed for a proper tripod grasp and smooth pen control—one fun activity at a time!

1. Sky Writing: Encourage your child to "write" letters or shapes in the air using their finger, a small stick, or even a magic wand! This helps them practice big movements that build muscle memory before transitioning to writing on paper.

2. Sensory Writing: Let your child trace letters and shapes in sand, salt, shaving cream, or finger paint. This tactile experience makes learning fun while strengthening their finger muscles and improving control.

3. Play-Dough Letters: Rolling, shaping, and pressing play-dough or clay into letter shapes helps strengthen hand muscles while reinforcing letter recognition. Bonus: Use alphabet cookie cutters for extra fun!

4. Pinch and Transfer Games: Using tweezers, clothespins, or tongs to pick up small objects like pom-poms or beads strengthens finger muscles and improves grip strength, which is essential for holding a pencil correctly.

5. Interlocking Blocks and Toys: Stacking and snapping together interlocking building blocks and toy pieces help develop hand strength, coordination, and problem-solving skills. The act of gripping and pressing pieces together strengthens the same muscles needed for proper pencil control.

Next, your child will begin their writing journey by tracing lines, patterns, and simple shapes. Ensure your child is gripping the pencil between their thumb and index finger. Their middle finger should curl up behind the pencil to support it. Their ring and pinky fingers should be tucked into their palms. This grip will help your child write smoothly and neatly.

Happy writing!

Pre-Writing Strokes

This first section is designed to help your child build a strong foundation for writing by practicing essential pre-writing strokes. Your child will start by tracing straight lines, diagonal lines, curved lines, shapes, and simple images. These exercises begin with short strokes and gradually increase in length and complexity to develop hand strength, coordination, and control. Each movement mimics those used in letter formation, making this step an important part of your child's handwriting journey.

We recommend using tools that support proper grip, such as golf pencils, short markers, or chunky crayons. These are easier for small hands to manage and naturally encourage a tripod grasp, where the pencil is held between the thumb, index, and middle fingers. This grasp gives children better control and helps prevent fatigue.

Good writing starts with proper hand form. Teach your child to lightly pinch the writing tool between their thumb and first finger and rest it on the middle finger. If they struggle, model the correct grip, use broken crayons or pencil grips, and offer hand-over-hand support when needed. Tracing shapes like circles, squares, and triangles helps children recognize patterns and prepares them for forming letters. Tracing images such as animals or objects adds fun and creativity while strengthening fine motor skills.

Focus on directionality as your child traces—moving from top to bottom and left to right. Following these patterns builds habits that support both writing and reading development. Curved strokes should be completed in one smooth motion, and arrows can guide direction.

Be patient and encouraging. Celebrate effort over perfection. Repetition builds muscle memory, and small victories lead to big progress. Allow your child to work at their own pace, repeat pages as needed, and have fun along the way. With your support, your child is building more than writing skills—they're gaining confidence and a love for learning.

Let's begin—one stroke, one shape, and one image at a time!

Start at the smiley face. Trace the dotted line. Use the arrow as a guide.

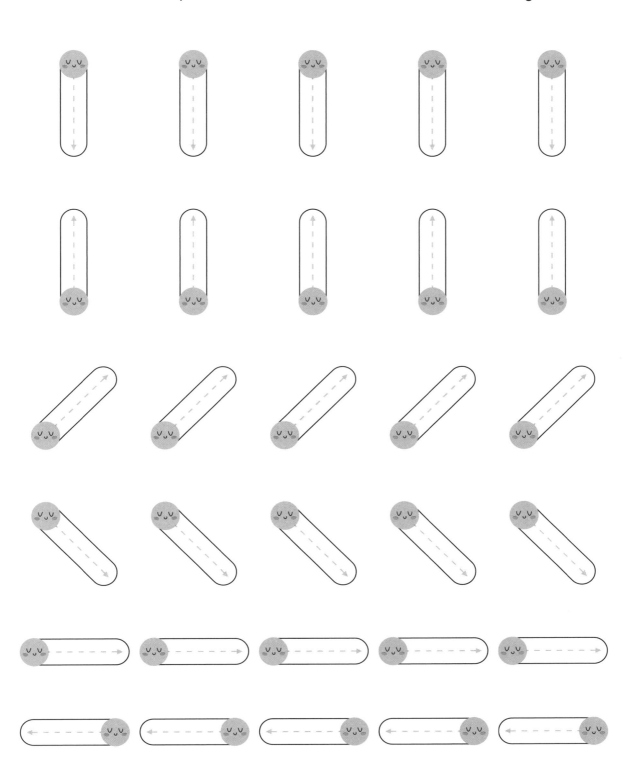

Start at the smiley face. Trace the dotted line and follow the arrows.

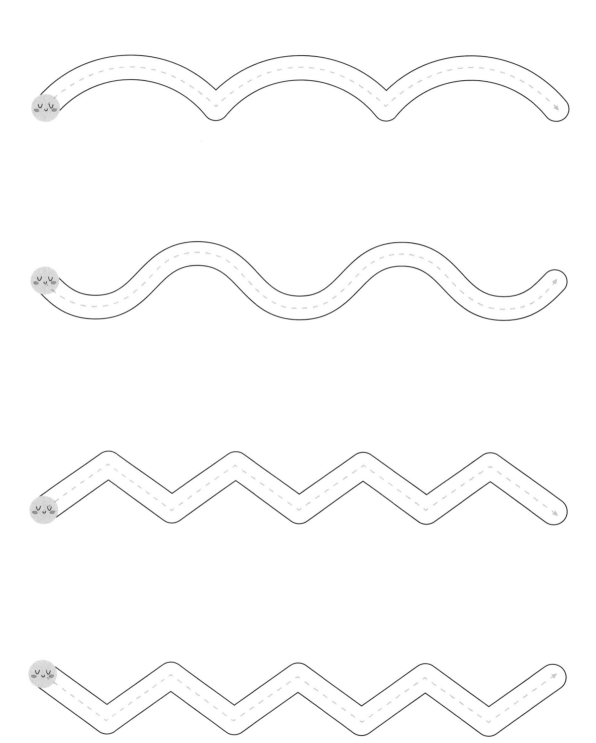

Start at the smiley face. Trace the dotted line and follow the arrows.

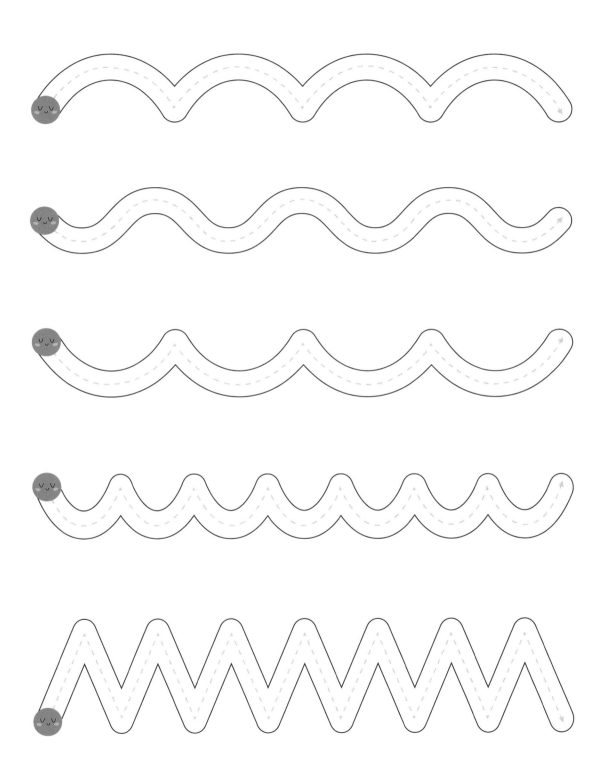

Trace the path. Help the bird find its nest.

Trace each shape.

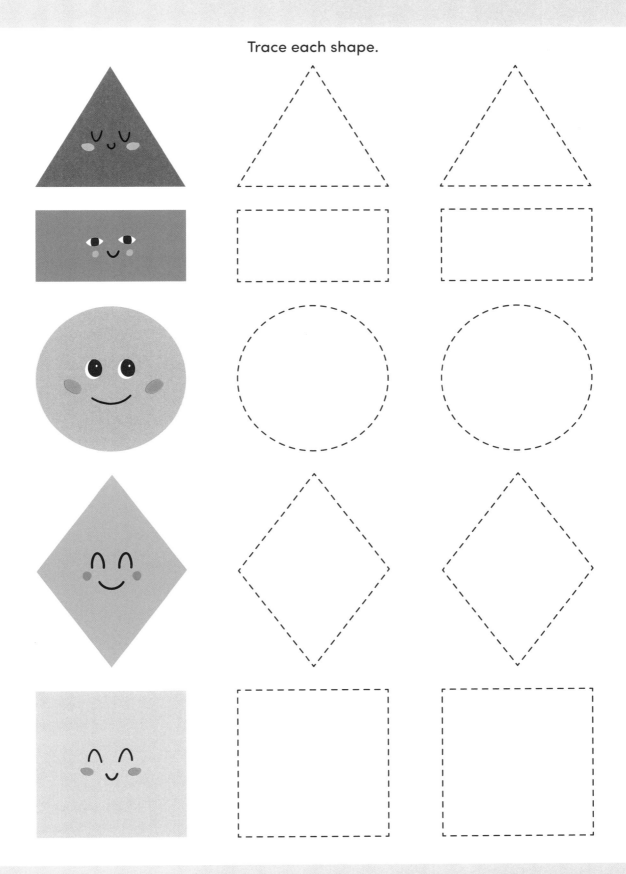

Trace and color the pictures. Circle your favorite sport.

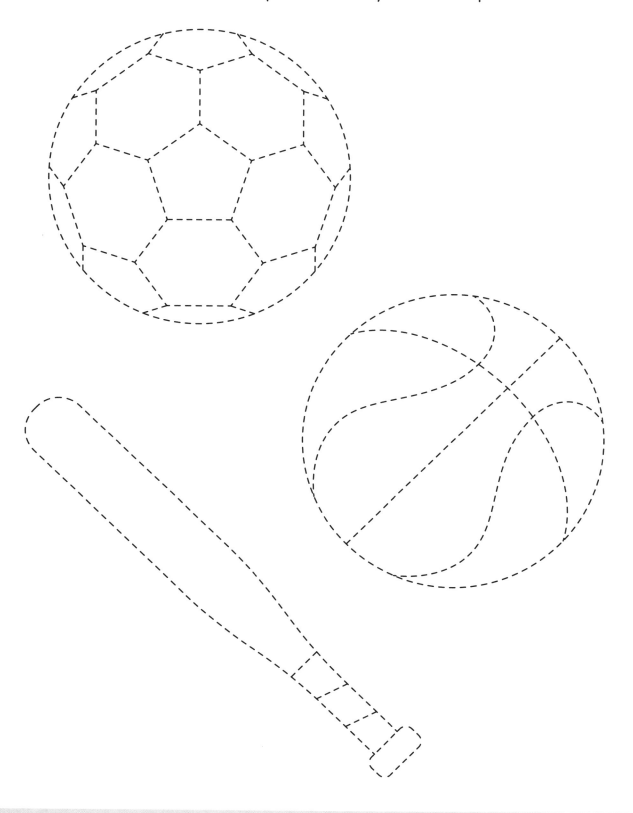

Letters, Sounds, and Tracing Practice

This section builds on foundational pre-writing skills by introducing letters, beginning sounds, and word-tracing activities. These engaging pages are designed to strengthen letter recognition, phonemic awareness (the ability to hear and work with the individual sounds in words), and proper handwriting habits—all in a fun and developmentally appropriate way.

Learners will focus on one letter at a time, beginning with uppercase and then moving to lowercase. Each letter is paired with a picture that starts with the same sound to help connect letters to words. Encourage saying the letter name and related word out loud to build both language and reading readiness.

LETTER TRACING

Children will trace uppercase and lowercase letters by following numbered arrows that guide proper stroke order. It's important to start at number 1 and follow each arrow carefully. Reinforce the habit of starting at the top and tracing slowly to build control and confidence. Each line includes multiple opportunities to practice.

USE THE RIGHT TOOLS

Continue offering short writing tools like golf pencils, short markers, or chunky crayons. These support the development of the tripod grasp, which helps build hand strength and writing control. If a learner struggles with grip, demonstrate the correct hold or try tools like pencil grips for support.

WORD TRACING AND MATCHING

This section also includes tracing simple words that begin with the focus letter (e.g., *ant*, *apple*, *ambulance*). First, trace the word together, then encourage the learner to write it independently. Matching pictures to words and hunting for letters provide a fun way to reinforce recognition and visual connection.

TIPS FOR SUCCESS

Encourage saying each letter and word aloud while working.

Remind the learner to trace slowly and with gentle pressure.

Allow time for coloring the images to increase engagement and fine motor practice.

This section lays the groundwork for reading and writing by blending movement, sound, and visuals. With your guidance and encouragement, learners will gain skills that lead to lifelong literacy. Remember to celebrate effort, not perfection. Let's keep learning—one letter at a time!

Alligator

 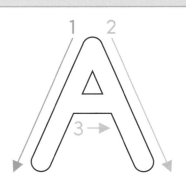

Trace the uppercase letter. Start at 1 and follow the arrows.

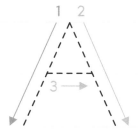 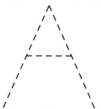 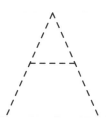 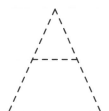

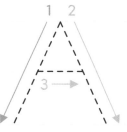   

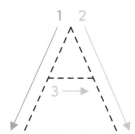 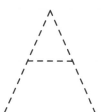 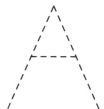 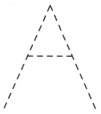

Color the images and say the words.

Apple

Ax

14

Trace the words. Start at 1 and follow the arrows. Say the words out loud.

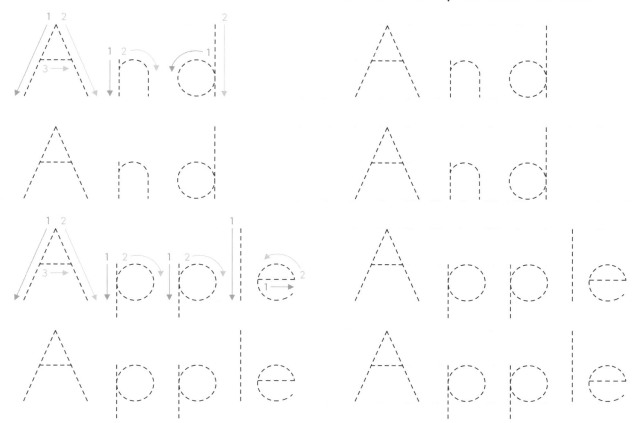

And And

And And

Apple Apple

Apple Apple

Find and circle each uppercase A.

A M A
X A K
V A Y

Match each picture to its word.

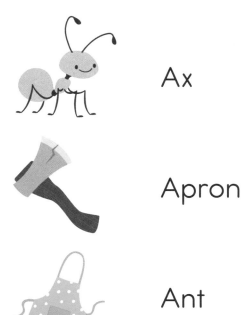

Ax

Apron

Ant

ant

 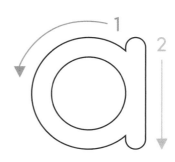

Trace the lowercase letter. Start at 1 and follow the arrows.

Look at the pictures and say the words.

ambulance   airplane   acorn

Fill in the missing lowercase letters. Say the words.

mbulance

irplane

corn

Trace the word. Start at 1 and follow the arrows.
Then, write the word on your own. Say the word out loud.

Find and circle each lowercase a.

d a a o a c g a a

17

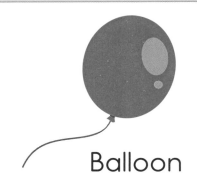

Balloon

Trace the uppercase letter. Start at 1 and follow the arrows.

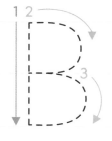   

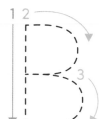   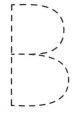

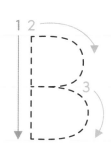   

Color the images and say the words.

Boat

Butterfly

Trace the words. Start at 1 and follow the arrows. Say the words out loud.

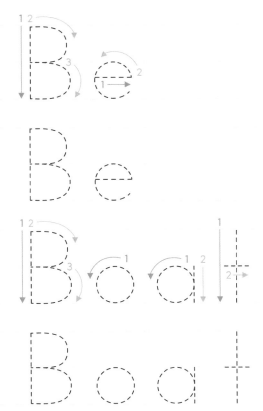
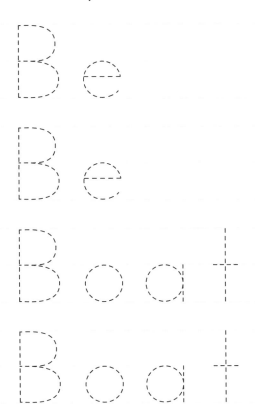

Find and circle each uppercase B.

R   P   B

D   B   E

B   F   B

Match each picture to its word.

   Bow

   Ball

   Bee

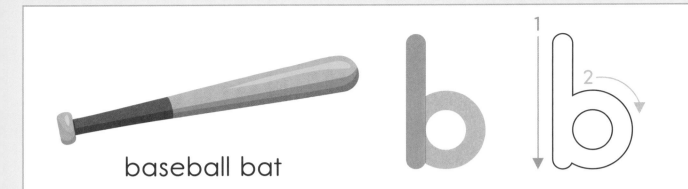

baseball bat

Trace the lowercase letter. Start at 1 and follow the arrows.

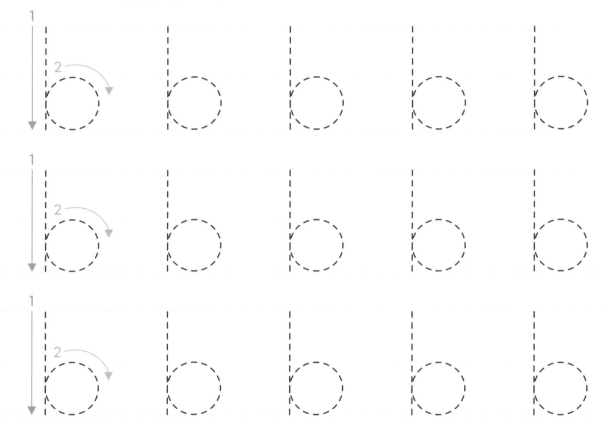

Look at the pictures and say the words.

bear

bandage

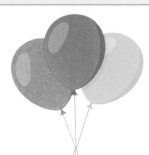

balloons

Fill in the missing lowercase letters. Say the words.

ear

andage

alloons

Trace the word. Start at 1 and follow the arrows.
Then, write the word on your own. Say the word out loud.

Find and circle each lowercase b.

a b d b b p b q b

Cupcake

 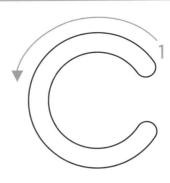

Trace the uppercase letter. Start at 1 and follow the arrow.

Color the images and say the words.

Crab

Cookie

Trace the words. Start at 1 and follow the arrows. Say the words out loud.

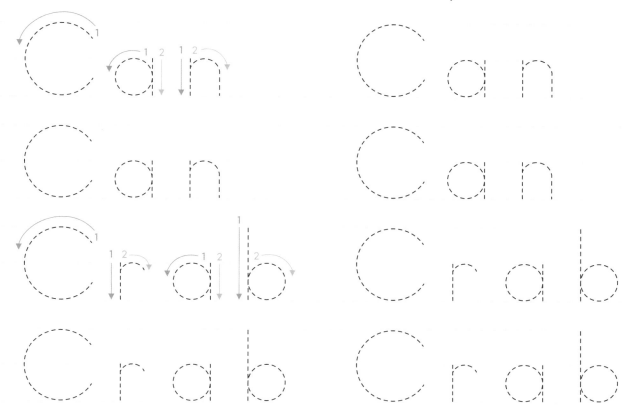

Can Can

Can Can

Crab Crab

Crab Crab

Find and circle each uppercase C.

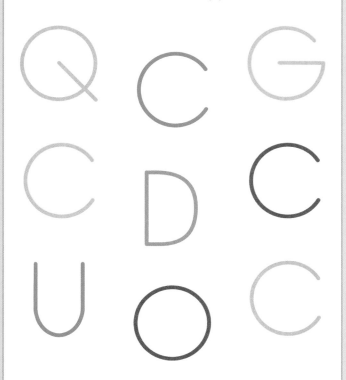

Q C G

C D C

U O C

Match each picture to its word.

Cow

Car

Cup

23

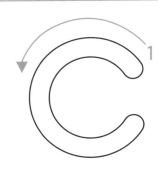

cactus

Trace the lowercase letter. Start at 1 and follow the arrow.

Look at the pictures and say the words.

castle   cake   cloud

Fill in the missing lowercase letters. Say the words.

astle

ake

loud

Trace the word. Start at 1 and follow the arrows.
Then, write the word on your own. Say the word out loud.

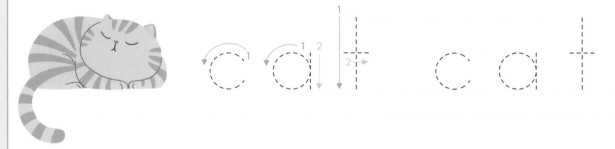

cat   cat

Find and circle each lowercase c.

c a e c c o c d c

Dinosaur

 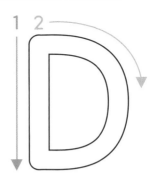

Trace the uppercase letter. Start at 1 and follow the arrows.

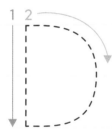   

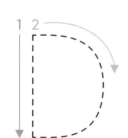   

Color the images and say the words.

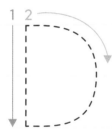

Dolphin

Dress

26

Trace the words. Start at 1 and follow the arrows. Say the words out loud.

Did Did

Did Did

Dress Dress

Dress Dress

Find and circle each uppercase D.

E U D

D P B

D D R

Match each picture to its word.

Drum

Dice

Dog

desk

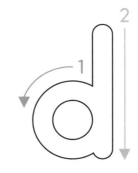

Trace the lowercase letter. Start at 1 and follow the arrows.

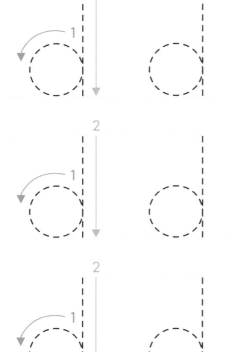

Look at the pictures and say the words.

donut

duck

daisy

Fill in the missing lowercase letters. Say the words.

 o n u t

 u c k

 a i s y

Trace the word. Start at 1 and follow the arrows.
Then, write the word on your own. Say the word out loud.

Find and circle each lowercase d.

b d p d d a d c d

Eight

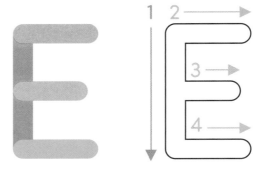

Trace the uppercase letter. Start at 1 and follow the arrows.

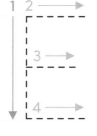   

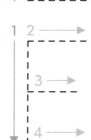  

Color the images and say the words.

Ear

Elephant

Trace the words. Start at 1 and follow the arrows. Say the words out loud.

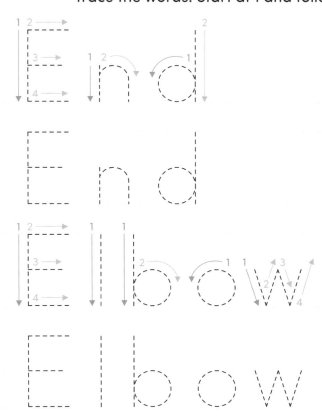
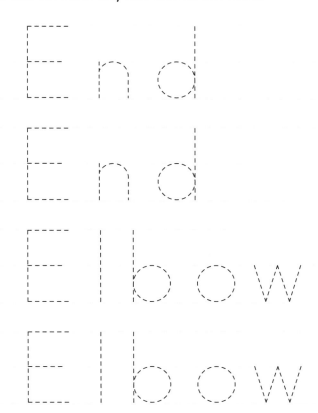

Find and circle each uppercase E.

B   E   T

R   E   E

E   F   N

Match each picture to its word.

   Ear

   Egg

   Elf

eye

Trace the lowercase letter. Start at 1 and follow the arrows.

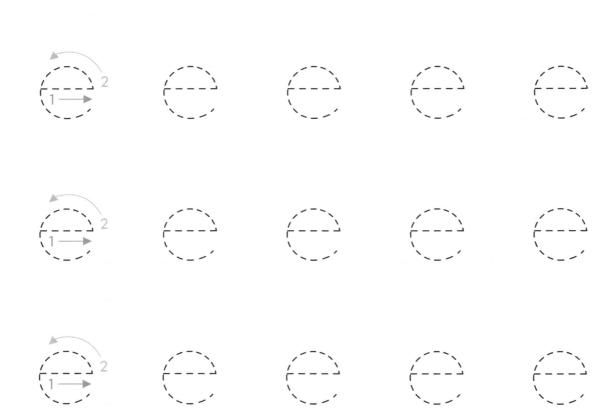

Look at the pictures and say the words.

envelope

eagle

eggplant

Fill in the missing lowercase letters. Say the words.

n v e l o p e

a g l e

g g p l a n t

Trace the word. Start at 1 and follow the arrows.
Then, write the word on your own. Say the word out loud.

Find and circle each lowercase e.

e   a   c   e   e   e   o   e   e   g

33

Football

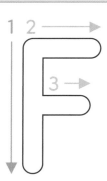

Trace the uppercase letter. Start at 1 and follow the arrows.

Color the images and say the words.

Frog

Farm

34

Trace the words. Start at 1 and follow the arrows. Say the words out loud.

Find and circle each uppercase F.

F	T	F
B	P	F
E	F	I

Match each picture to its word.

 Flag

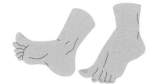 Fire

 Feet

35

fairy

 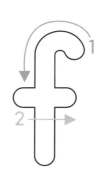

Trace the lowercase letter. Start at 1 and follow the arrows.

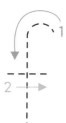    

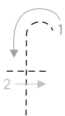    

Look at the pictures and say the words.

 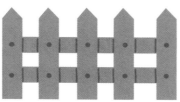 

fries   fence   fish

36

Fill in the missing lowercase letters. Say the words.

r i e s

e n c e

i s h

Trace the word. Start at 1 and follow the arrows.
Then, write the word on your own. Say the word out loud.

Find and circle each lowercase f.

f j f f f l f r

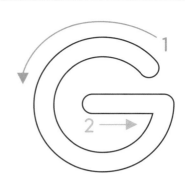

Globe

Trace the uppercase letter. Start at 1 and follow the arrows.

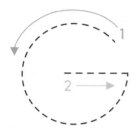
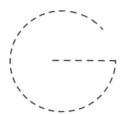
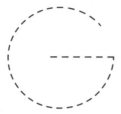
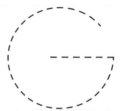

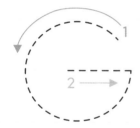

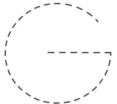
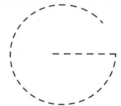

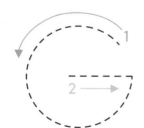

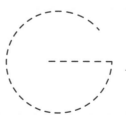
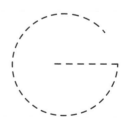

Color the images and say the words.

Goat

Grapes

Trace the words. Start at 1 and follow the arrows. Say the words out loud.

Find and circle each uppercase G.

G D U

Q G C

G O G

Match each picture to its word.

 Goat

 Glue

 Grass

gift

 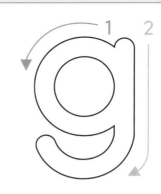

Trace the lowercase letter. Start at 1 and follow the arrows.

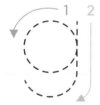

Look at the pictures and say the words.

guitar   gorilla   garbage

40

Fill in the missing lowercase letters. Say the words.

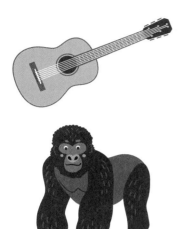

uitar

orilla

arbage

Trace the word. Start at 1 and follow the arrows.
Then, write the word on your own. Say the word out loud.

Find and circle each lowercase g.

g g a d g q g g p

Hamburger

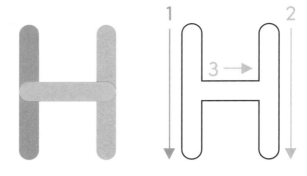

Trace the uppercase letter. Start at 1 and follow the arrows.

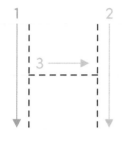 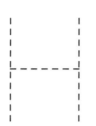  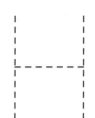

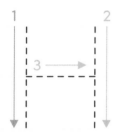  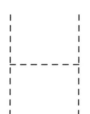 

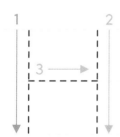   

Color the images and say the words.

Hippo

House

Trace the words. Start at 1 and follow the arrows. Say the words out loud.

Had   Had

Had   Had

Hippo   Hippo

Hippo   Hippo

Find and circle each uppercase H.

T F H

H E N

I H H

Match each picture to its word.

Hat

Horse

Hand

horse

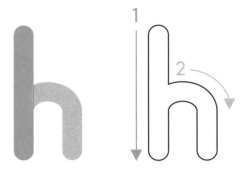

Trace the lowercase letter. Start at 1 and follow the arrows.

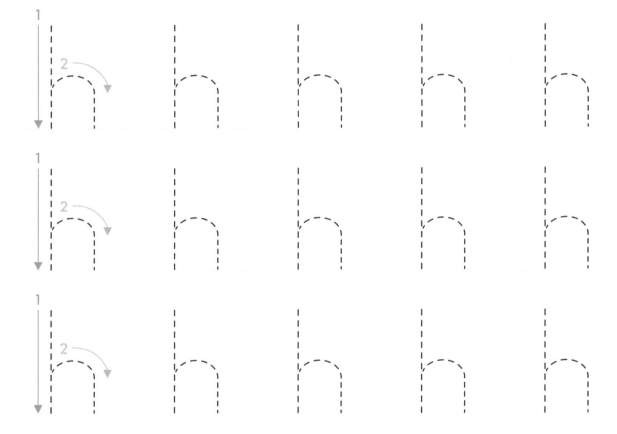

Look at the pictures and say the words.

hammer

hotdog

heart

Fill in the missing lowercase letters. Say the words.

 ammer

 otdog

 eart

Trace the word. Start at 1 and follow the arrows.
Then, write the word on your own. Say the word out loud.

 hen    hen

Find and circle each lowercase h.

h   b   r   h   l   h   h   n

  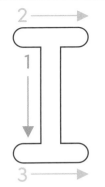

Iguana

Trace the uppercase letter. Start at 1 and follow the arrows.

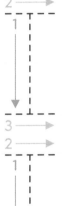   

Color the images and say the words.

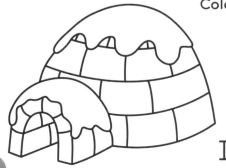

Igloo

Ice cream

Trace the words. Start at 1 and follow the arrows. Say the words out loud.

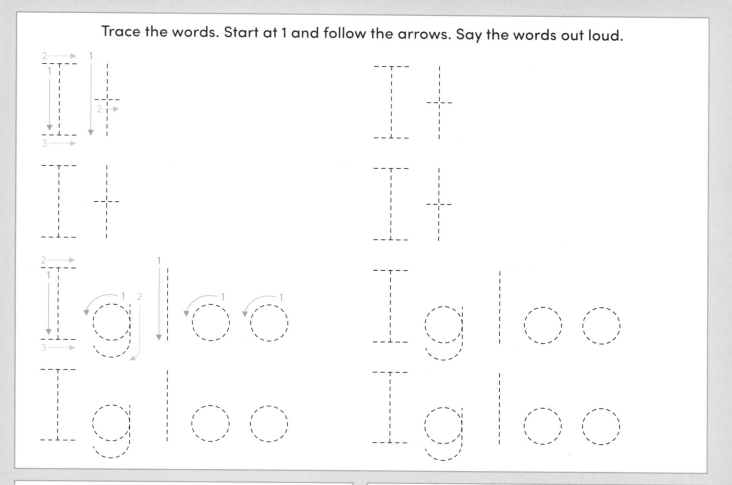

Find and circle each uppercase I.

H T F

I L N

I L I

Match each picture to its word.

Island

Ice

Igloo

inchworm

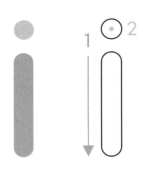

Trace the lowercase letter. Start at 1 and follow the arrows.

1 2

1 2

1 2

Look at the pictures and say the words.

iguana

inchworm

ice skate

Fill in the missing lowercase letters. Say the words.

 guana

 nchworm

 ce skate

Trace the word. Start at 1 and follow the arrows.
Then, write the word on your own. Say the word out loud.

 ice ice

Find and circle each lowercase i.

i j l t i i r i i

Jellyfish

 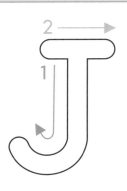

Trace the uppercase letter. Start at 1 and follow the arrows.

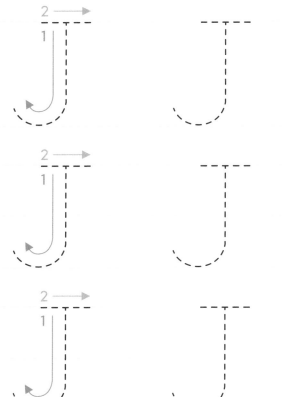

Color the images and say the words.

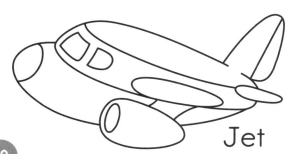

Jet

Jellybeans

Trace the words. Start at 1 and follow the arrows. Say the words out loud.

Find and circle each uppercase J.

Match each picture to its word.

Jacket

Jar

Jam

jam

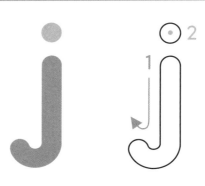

Trace the lowercase letter. Start at 1 and follow the arrows.

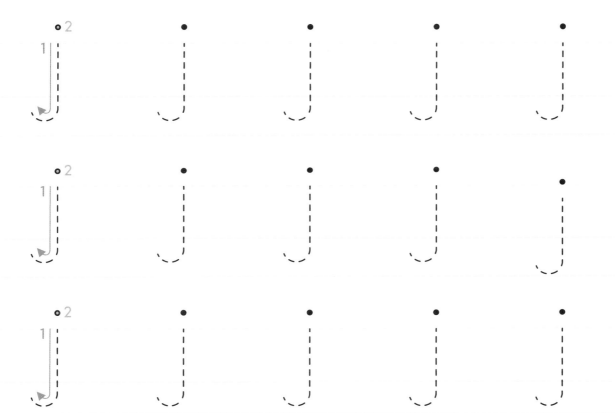

Look at the pictures and say the words.

juggle

juice

jewelry

Fill in the missing lowercase letters. Say the words.

uggle

uice

ewelry

Trace the word. Start at 1 and follow the arrows.
Then, write the word on your own. Say the word out loud.

Find and circle each lowercase j.

l   f   j         j   r   j

Koala

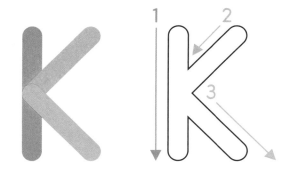

Trace the uppercase letter. Start at 1 and follow the arrows.

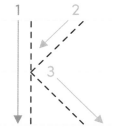 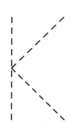 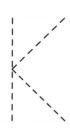 

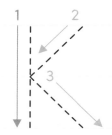   

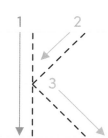   

Color the images and say the words.

King

Kangaroo

54

Trace the words. Start at 1 and follow the arrows. Say the words out loud.

Kit   Kit

Kit   Kit

King   King

King   King

Find and circle each uppercase K.

K R K

Z I F

K H K

Match each picture to its word.

 Kiwi

 Kiss

 Key

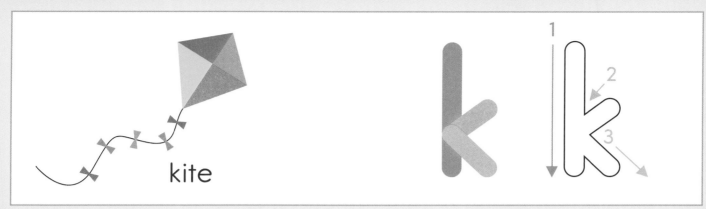

kite

Trace the lowercase letter. Start at 1 and follow the arrows.

k k k k k

k k k k k

k k k k k

Look at the pictures and say the words.

kayak

king

karate

Fill in the missing lowercase letters. Say the words.

 ayak

 ing

 arate

Trace the word. Start at 1 and follow the arrows.
Then, write the word on your own. Say the word out loud.

 kiwi kiwi

Find and circle each lowercase k.

k k h x l k k y k

Ladybug

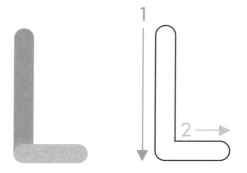

Trace the uppercase letter. Start at 1 and follow the arrows.

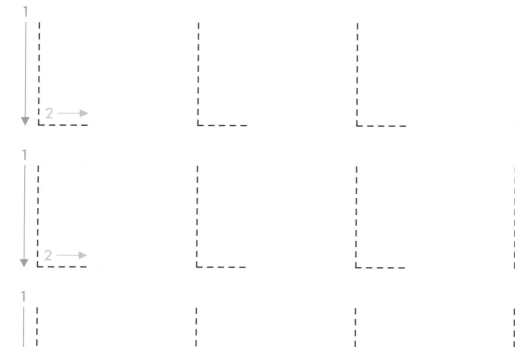

Color the images and say the words.

Lion

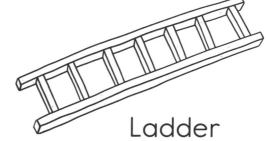

Ladder

Trace the words. Start at 1 and follow the arrows. Say the words out loud.

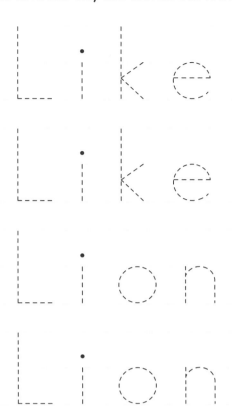

Find and circle each uppercase L.

L T L

H L F

L I J

Match each picture to its word.

   Light

   Lock

   Lime

lemon

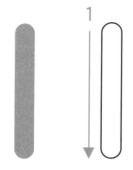

Trace the lowercase letter. Start at 1 and follow the arrow.

1

1

1

Look at the pictures and say the words.

lemon

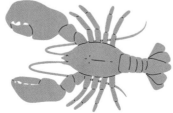

lobster

leaf

60

Fill in the missing lowercase letters. Say the words.

 e m o n

 o b s t e r

 e a f

Trace the word. Start at 1 and follow the arrows.
Then, write the word on your own. Say the word out loud.

  l o g

Find and circle each lowercase i.

 i l l k l j h l l

Mailbox

Trace the uppercase letter. Start at 1 and follow the arrows.

Color the images and say the words.

Muffin

Mirror

Trace the words. Start at 1 and follow the arrows. Say the words out loud.

Find and circle each uppercase M.

M N M

X H M

M W V

Match each picture to its word.

Milk

Map

Moon

money

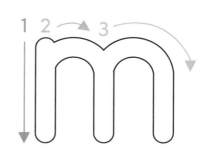

Trace the lowercase letter. Start at 1 and follow the arrows.

Look at the pictures and say the words.

monkey

mountain

mermaid

Fill in the missing lowercase letters. Say the words.

onkey

ountain

ermaid

Trace the word. Start at 1 and follow the arrows.
Then, write the word on your own. Say the word out loud.

Find and circle each lowercase m.

m n r m m W m h m

Necklace

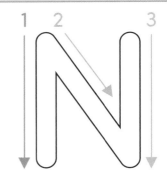

Trace the uppercase letter. Start at 1 and follow the arrows.

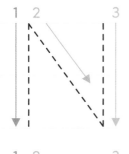 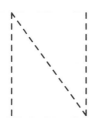 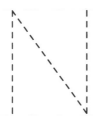 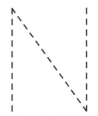

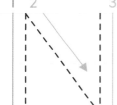 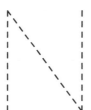 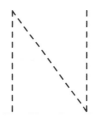 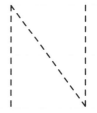

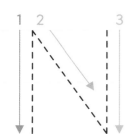 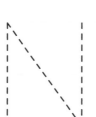 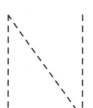 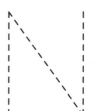

Color the images and say the words.

Nest

Nine

Trace the words. Start at 1 and follow the arrows. Say the words out loud.

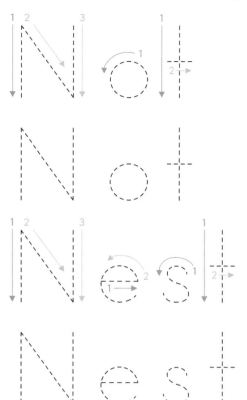

Not   Not

Not   Not

Nest   Nest

Nest   Nest

Find and circle each uppercase N.

N Z N

H N X

M V N

Match each picture to its word.

   Nine

   Nail

   Nut

nose

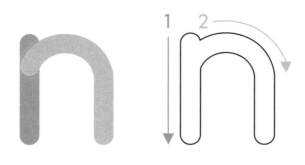

Trace the lowercase letter. Start at 1 and follow the arrows.

Look at the pictures and say the words.

notebook

narwhal

net

68

Fill in the missing lowercase letters. Say the words.

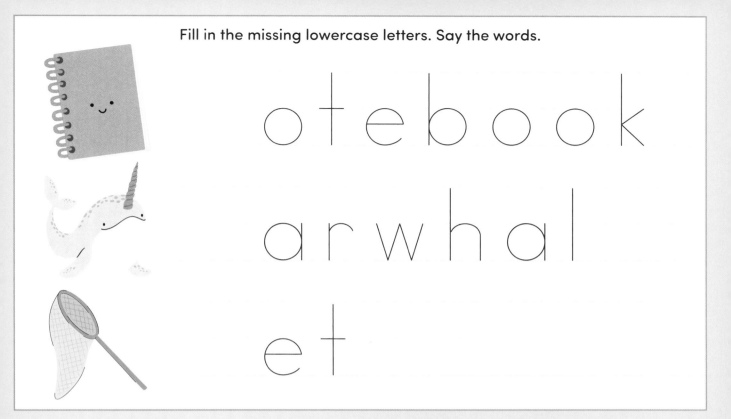

otebook

arwhal

et

Trace the word. Start at 1 and follow the arrows.
Then, write the word on your own. Say the word out loud.

 net   net

Find and circle each lowercase n.

h n r n m n n u n

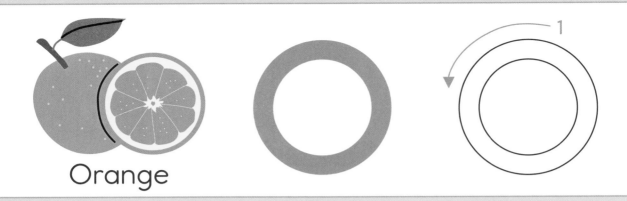

Orange

Trace the uppercase letter. Start at 1 and follow the arrow.

Color the images and say the words.

Oven

Ostrich

70

Trace the words. Start at 1 and follow the arrows. Say the words out loud.

Find and circle each uppercase O.

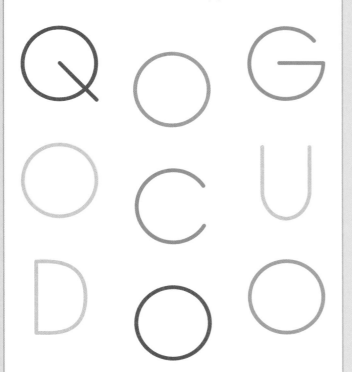

Match each picture to its word.

Oven

Owl

Ostrich

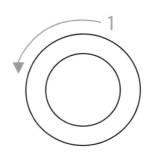

onion

Trace the lowercase letter. Start at 1 and follow the arrow.

Look at the pictures and say the words.

octopus

oyster

one

Fill in the missing lowercase letters. Say the words.

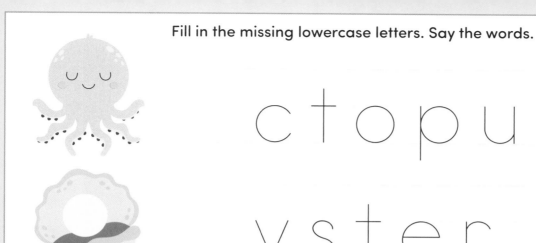

_ctopus

_yster

_ne

Trace the word. Start at 1 and follow the arrows.
Then, write the word on your own. Say the word out loud.

 owl   owl

Find and circle each lowercase o.

q o o o c o g a o o

Plant

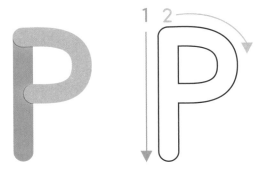

Trace the uppercase letter. Start at 1 and follow the arrows.

Color the images and say the words.

Pie

Purse

Trace the words. Start at 1 and follow the arrows. Say the words out loud.

Find and circle each uppercase P.

P E D

B P F

P R P

Match each picture to its word.

 Peas

 Paint

 Panda

pizza

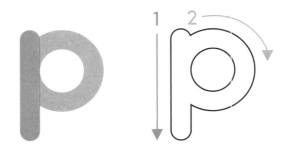

Trace the lowercase letter. Start at 1 and follow the arrows.

Look at the pictures and say the words.

pencil

popcorn

penguin

Fill in the missing lowercase letters. Say the words.

encil

opcorn

enguin

Trace the word. Start at 1 and follow the arrows.
Then, write the word on your own. Say the word out loud.

Find and circle each lowercase p.

q b p p d p g p

Quilt

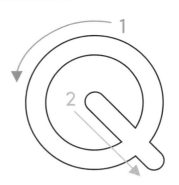

Trace the uppercase letter. Start at 1 and follow the arrows.

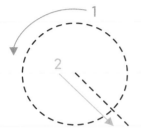   

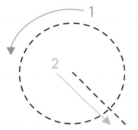   

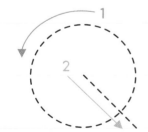   

Color the images and say the words.

Queen

Quarter

Trace the words. Start at 1 and follow the arrows. Say the words out loud.

Quit   Quit

Quit   Quit

Queen   Queen

Queen   Queen

Find and circle each uppercase Q.

Q   C   Q

U   Q   O

G   Q   Q

Match each picture to its word.

Quarter

Queen

Quilt

quiz

Trace the lowercase letter. Start at 1 and follow the arrows.

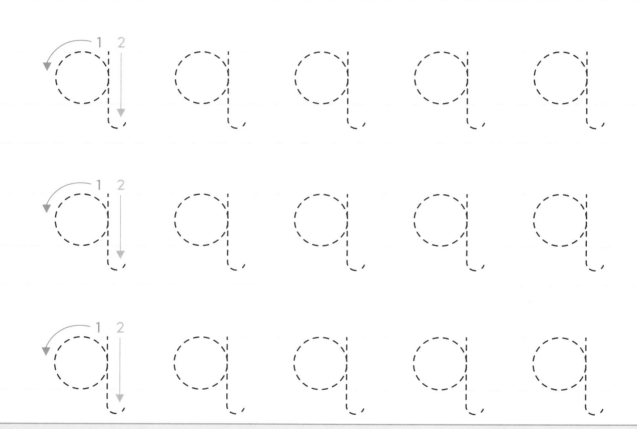

Look at the pictures and say the words.

question   quiet   quartz

Fill in the missing lowercase letters. Say the words.

uestion

uiet

uartz

Trace the word. Start at 1 and follow the arrows.
Then, write the word on your own. Say the word out loud.

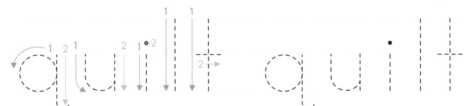

Find and circle each lowercase q.

q b a q d a g q p

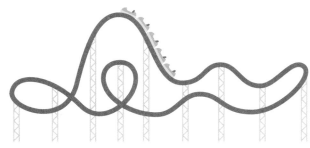

Roller coaster

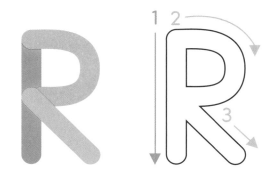

Trace the uppercase letter. Start at 1 and follow the arrows.

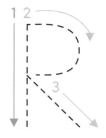   

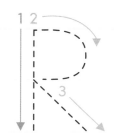   

Color the images and say the words.

 Rainbow

 Radio

Trace the words. Start at 1 and follow the arrows. Say the words out loud.

Run

Run

Radio

Radio

Find and circle each uppercase R.

R E R

B R F

P R R

Match each picture to its word.

Rat

Ruler

Ring

rain

Trace the lowercase letter. Start at 1 and follow the arrows.

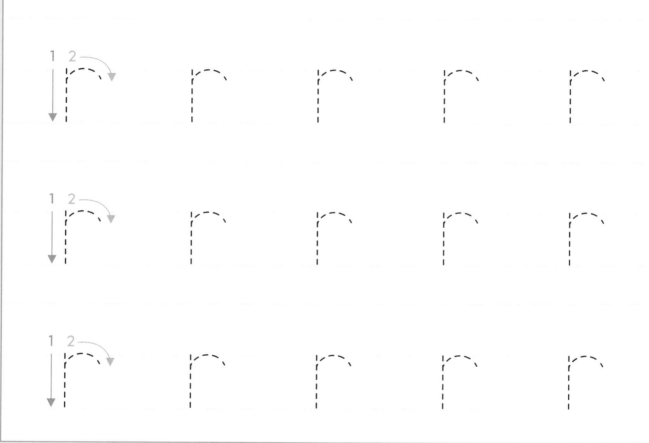

Look at the pictures and say the words.

robot

rocket

rabbit

Fill in the missing lowercase letters. Say the words.

o b o t

o c k e t

a b b i t

Trace the word. Start at 1 and follow the arrows.
Then, write the word on your own. Say the word out loud.

r u g   r u g

Find and circle each lowercase r.

r m r n h r r u r

 Seahorse

Trace the uppercase letter. Start at 1 and follow the arrow.

Color the images and say the words.

 Sun

 Scissors

Trace the words. Start at 1 and follow the arrows. Say the words out loud.

Find and circle each uppercase S.

S S B

P R S

D S J

Match each picture to its word.

 Square

 Shell

 Snail

snake

Trace the lowercase letter. Start at 1 and follow the arrow.

Look at the pictures and say the words.

strawberry

star

sunflower

Fill in the missing lowercase letters. Say the words.

_trawberry

_tar

_unflower

Trace the word. Start at 1 and follow the arrows.
Then, write the word on your own. Say the word out loud.

s u b   s u b

Find and circle each lowercase s.

s   s   e   s   f   S   g   j   s

Table

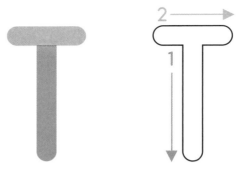

Trace the uppercase letter. Start at 1 and follow the arrows.

Color the images and say the words.

Tree

Tractor

Trace the words. Start at 1 and follow the arrows. Say the words out loud.

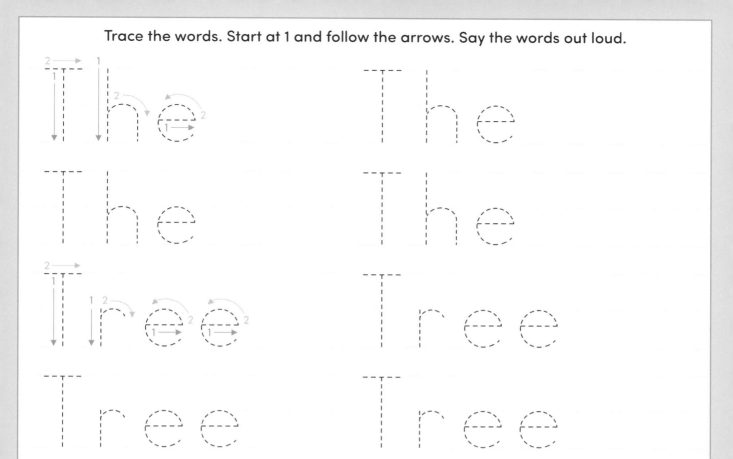

The
The
Tree
Tree

The
The
Tree
Tree

Find and circle each uppercase T.

E T T
E T T
T L F
I T J

Match each picture to its word.

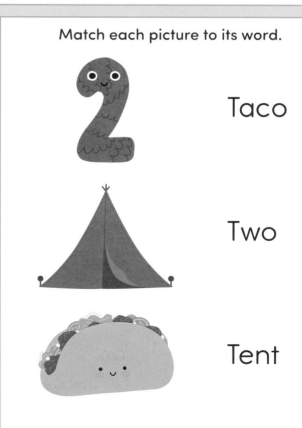

Taco

Two

Tent

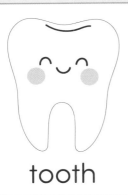

tooth

 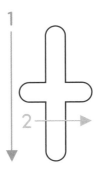

Trace the lowercase letter. Start at 1 and follow the arrows.

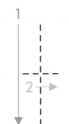   

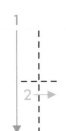    

Look at the pictures and say the words.

truck   two   tiger

Fill in the missing lowercase letters. Say the words.

r u c k

w o

i g e r

Trace the word. Start at 1 and follow the arrows.
Then, write the word on your own. Say the word out loud.

Find and circle each lowercase t.

t   k   t   t   f   t   r   t   l

Unicorn

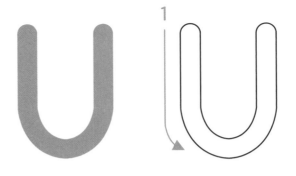

Trace the uppercase letter. Start at 1 and follow the arrow.

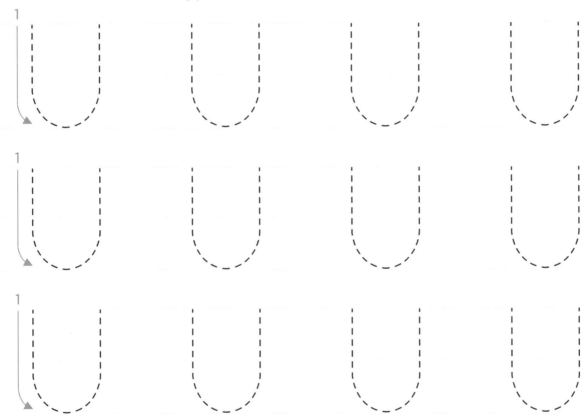

Color the images and say the words.

Up

Umbrella

Trace the words. Start at 1 and follow the arrows. Say the words out loud.

Us Us

Us Us

Urchin Urchin

Urchin Urchin

Find and circle each uppercase U.

R U J

D U S

U V U

Match each picture to its word.

Umbrella

Under

Up

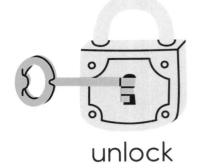

unlock

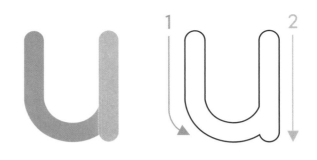

Trace the lowercase letter. Start at 1 and follow the arrows.

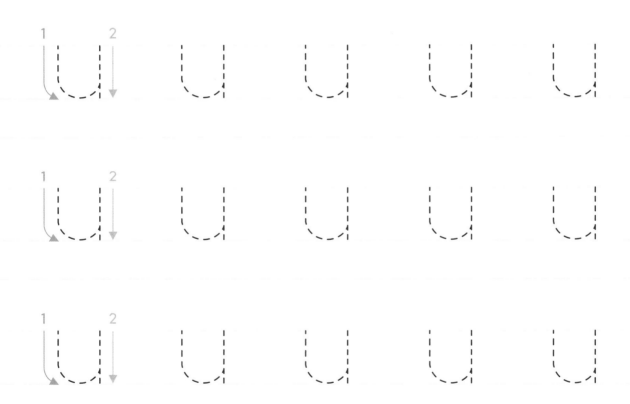

Look at the pictures and say the words.

underwear

unicorn

umpire

Fill in the missing lowercase letters. Say the words.

nderwear

nicorn

mpire

Trace the word. Start at 1 and follow the arrows.
Then, write the word on your own. Say the word out loud.

Find and circle each lowercase u.

u v u n m u r u u

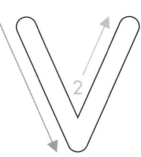

Volleyball

Trace the uppercase letter. Start at 1 and follow the arrows.

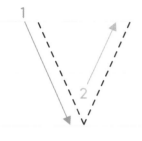   

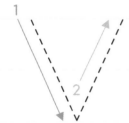   

Color the images and say the words.

Volcano

Vest

Trace the words. Start at 1 and follow the arrows. Say the words out loud.

Find and circle each uppercase V.

Match each picture to its word.

 Vase

 Violin

 Van

99

vulture

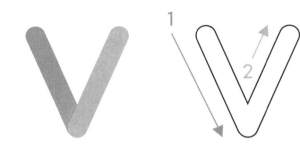

Trace the lowercase letter. Start at 1 and follow the arrows.

Look at the pictures and say the words.

vacuum   vegetables   video game

Fill in the missing lowercase letters. Say the words.

 a c u u m

 egetables

 ideo games

---

Trace the word. Start at 1 and follow the arrows.
Then, write the word on your own. Say the word out loud.

  vet  vet

---

Find and circle each lowercase v.

k v u v z v w v

Window

 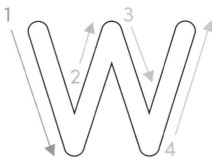

Trace the uppercase letter. Start at 1 and follow the arrows.

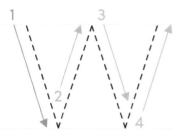 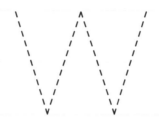 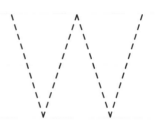

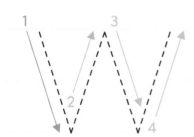 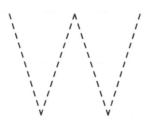 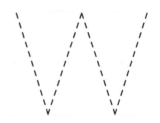

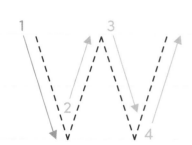  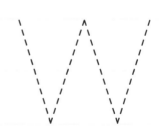

Color the images and say the words.

Worm

Whale

Trace the words. Start at 1 and follow the arrows. Say the words out loud.

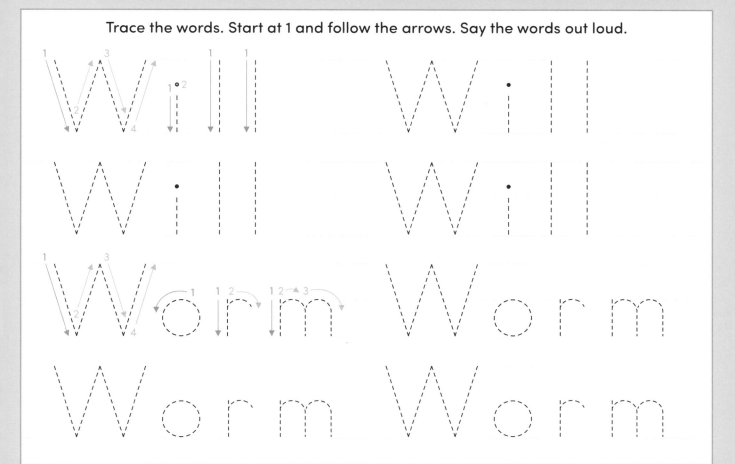

Find and circle each uppercase W.

Match each picture to its word.

Worm

Whale

Window

wagon

Trace the lowercase letter. Start at 1 and follow the arrows.

Look at the pictures and say the words.

watch

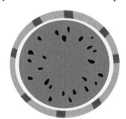

watermelon

wheel

Fill in the missing lowercase letters. Say the words.

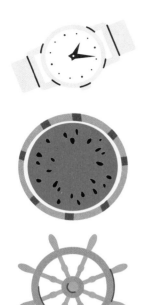

atch

atermelon

heel

Trace the word. Start at 1 and follow the arrows.
Then, write the word on your own. Say the word out loud.

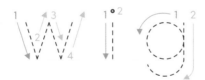 

Find and circle each lowercase w.

w W k w z v W w y

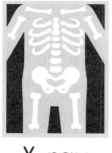

X-ray

Trace the uppercase letter. Start at 1 and follow the arrows.

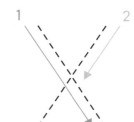   

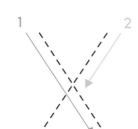   

Color the images and say the words.

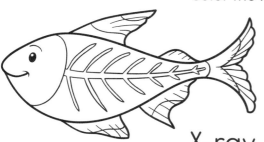

X-ray fish

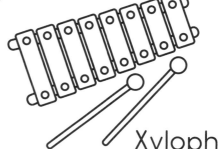

Xylophone

Trace the words. Start at 1 and follow the arrows. Say the words out loud.

Find and circle each uppercase X.

Match each picture to its word.

 X-ray fish

 fox

 taxi

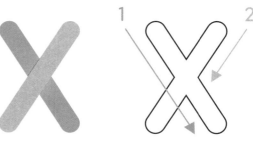

x-ray fish

Trace the lowercase letter. Start at 1 and follow the arrows.

Look at the pictures and say the words.

mixer

ox

xylophone

Fill in the missing lowercase letters. Say the words.

mi_er

o_

_ylophone

Trace the word. Start at 1 and follow the arrows.
Then, write the word on your own. Say the word out loud.

Find and circle each lowercase x.

 x k x x z   x x y

Yogurt

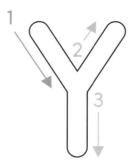

Trace the uppercase letter. Start at 1 and follow the arrows.

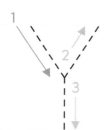   

Color the images and say the words.

Yoga

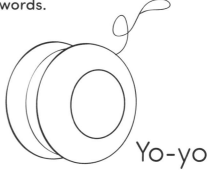

Yo-yo

Trace the words. Start at 1 and follow the arrows. Say the words out loud.

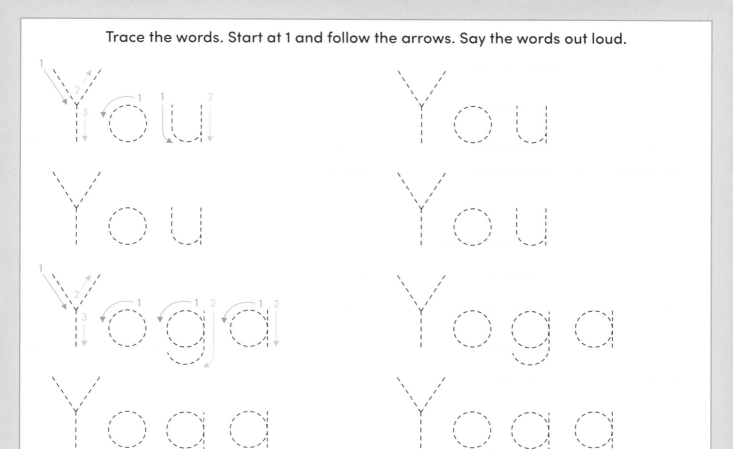

Find and circle each uppercase Y.

Match each picture to its word.

Yogurt

Yo-yo

Yoga

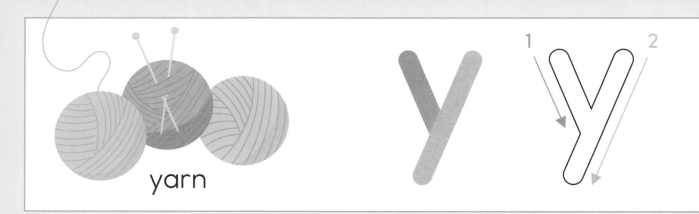

yarn

y y

Trace the lowercase letter. Start at 1 and follow the arrows.

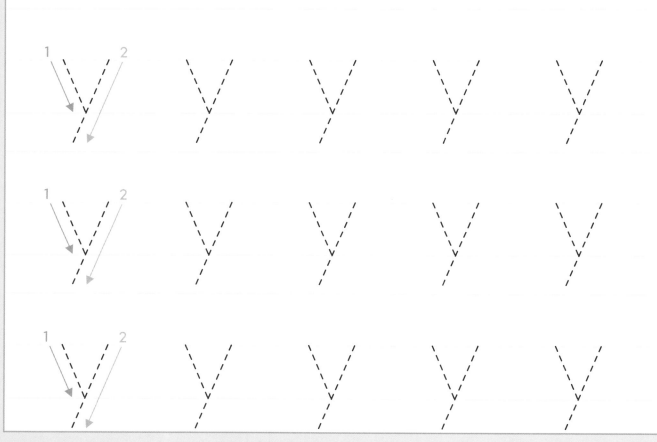

Look at the pictures and say the words.

yam

yak

yeti

Fill in the missing lowercase letters. Say the words.

a m

a k

e t i

Trace the word. Start at 1 and follow the arrows.
Then, write the word on your own. Say the word out loud.

y a m   y a m

Find and circle each lowercase y.

y k y y t y Y l x y

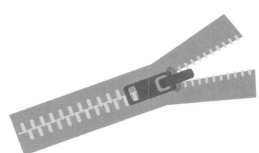

Zipper

Trace the uppercase letter. Start at 1 and follow the arrows.

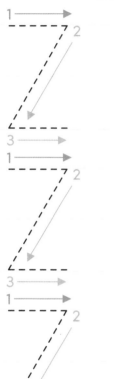

Color the images and say the words.

Zebra

Zoo

Trace the words. Start at 1 and follow the arrows. Say the words out loud.

Find and circle each uppercase Z.

X Z Z

Z Y F

I N Z

Match each picture to its word.

Zebra

Zipper

Zero

zigzag

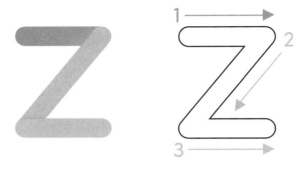

Trace the lowercase letter. Start at 1 and follow the arrows.

Look at the pictures and say the words.

zebra

zero

zigzag

Fill in the missing lowercase letters. Say the words.

e b r a

e r o

i g z a g

Trace the word. Start at 1 and follow the arrows.
Then, write the word on your own. Say the word out loud.

 z o o

Find and circle each lowercase z.

z v t z z y x z z

Sight Words and CVC Word Practice

In this section of the workbook, learners will begin working with sight words and CVC words—two important building blocks for early reading and writing development. These pages help build fluency, confidence, and comprehension through visual recognition, sound blending, and writing practice.

WHAT ARE SIGHT WORDS?

Sight words are common words children should recognize instantly without sounding out (e.g., *the, can, go, see, it*). These words often don't follow phonics rules, and appear frequently in texts. Recognizing them by sight helps learners read more smoothly and understand what they're reading.

WHAT ARE CVC WORDS?

CVC stands for *consonant–vowel–consonant*. These are short words like *cat, dog, bat,* and *sit* that follow regular spelling patterns and can be sounded out. Practicing them helps learners understand how letters form words, strengthening both phonics and spelling.

ACTIVITIES IN THIS SECTION

Word Picture Match: Learners look at an image and choose the correct word, building visual recognition and vocabulary.

Word Hunts: Learners search for specific sight words and circle them, reinforcing memory and word identification.

Tracing Practice: Sight words and CVC words are traced with dotted lines to build fine motor skills and reinforce spelling patterns.

Repetition and Variety: Each word is practiced several times to build muscle memory and support retention.

TIPS FOR HOME SUPPORT

Encourage learners to say each word out loud as they trace or find it.

Reinforce beginning sounds and letter-sound patterns.

Praise effort and progress, even when it's not perfect.

Revisit tricky words and let learners go at their own pace.

By working with both sight words and CVC words regularly, learners strengthen essential literacy skills, preparing them to become confident independent readers and writers.

Trace the sight words.

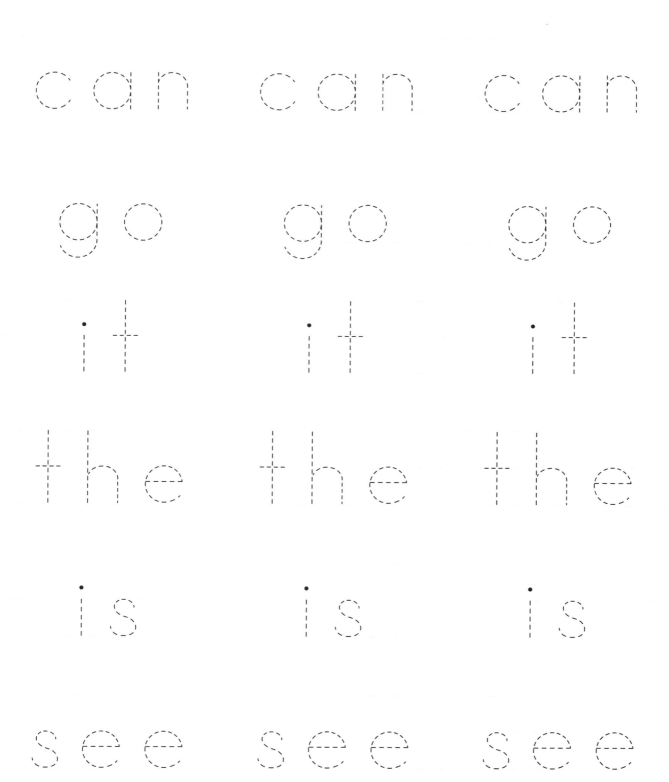

can   can   can

go   go   go

it   it   it

the   the   the

is   is   is

see   see   see

Trace the sight words.

like   like   like

you   you   you

and   and   and

to   to   to

not   not   not

look   look   look

Trace the sight words.

for for for

too too too

she she she

we we we

no no no

will will will

Trace the sight words.

all   all   all

did   did   did

are   are   are

get   get   get

do   do   do

with   with   with

Find and circle these sight words.

can like the see go

see

cat   can

can   net

met   sit

like

the   go

dog   ten

hit   see   the

go   like

pig

cup   cup   cup

bat   bat   bat

net   net   net

mat   mat   mat

sit   sit   sit

dog   dog   dog

Trace the CVC words.

hug hug hug

man man man

ten ten ten

fun fun fun

kid kid kid

not not not

Trace the CVC words.

rug rug rug

ham ham ham

hen hen hen

bib bib bib

lip lip lip

pot pot pot

Trace the sight words.

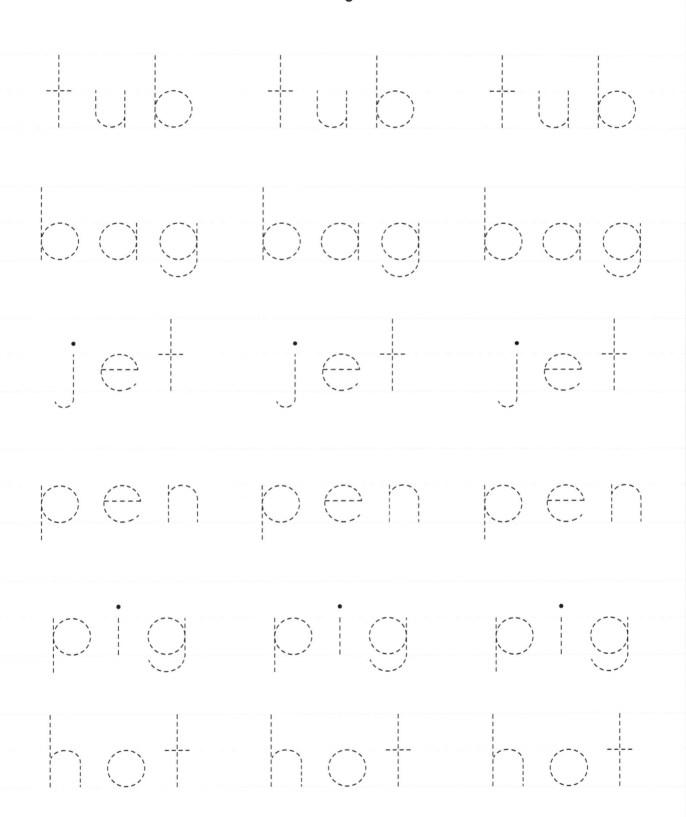

Circle the correct word.

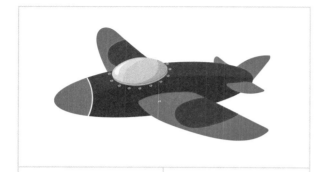

jet | jar

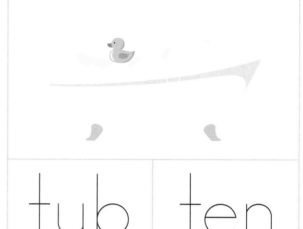

tub | ten

dug | dog

can | cat

rug | rat

cup | cat

Number Practice (0 to 10)

Welcome to the number practice section of *Big Handwriting Practice Workbook for Kids*! In this part of the workbook, learners will explore and practice writing numbers from zero to ten. These pages are designed to support number recognition, counting skills, and proper number formation through visual, tactile, and written activities.

Each number is introduced with a numeral, the number word, counting visuals (like bears or objects), and tracing lines that guide learners through correct number formation using arrows and numbered steps. Learners will also engage in simple counting prompts that encourage them to count aloud and connect quantities to written numbers.

These activities combine fine motor development with early math readiness skills. Tracing numbers helps strengthen hand muscles while reinforcing directionality and consistency in number writing. Visual supports like ten frames and objects allow learners to build a clear understanding of number value and quantity.

TIPS FOR SUCCESS

Encourage learners to use their finger to trace the large number and say it out loud before writing.

Practice counting the images together and relate them to the numeral shown.

Remind learners to start at the top and follow the directional arrows when tracing numbers.

Use positive reinforcement and let learners repeat pages as needed for extra confidence.

By practicing numbers in multiple ways—visually, verbally, and kinesthetically—learners build a strong math foundation. Let's dive in and make number learning fun and meaningful!

zero

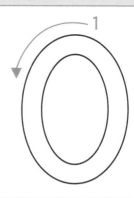

Trace the number. Start at 1 and follow the arrow.

   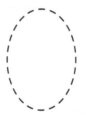 

How many scoops of ice cream
are on the cone?

Use your finger to trace the number
and say the number out loud.

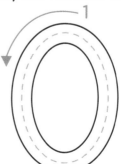

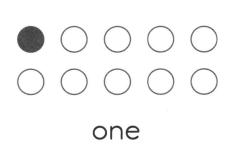

one

Trace the number. Start at 1 and follow the arrows.

How many bows are on the bear?

Use your finger to trace the number and say the number out loud.

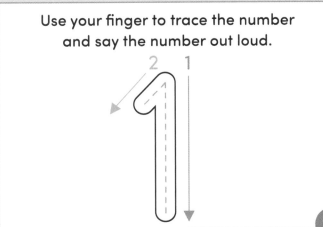

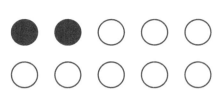

two

Trace the number. Start at 1 and follow the arrows.

How many fish are in the tank?

Use your finger to trace the number and say the number out loud.

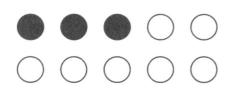

three

Trace the number. Start at 1 and follow the arrows.

How many apples are on the tree?

Use your finger to trace the number and say the number out loud.

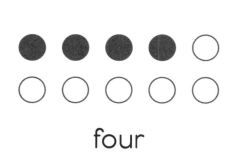

four

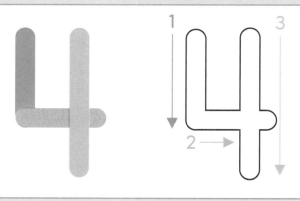

Trace the number. Start at 1 and follow the arrows.

How many flowers are on the vine?

Use your finger to trace the number and say the number out loud.

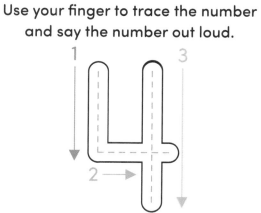

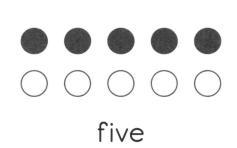

five

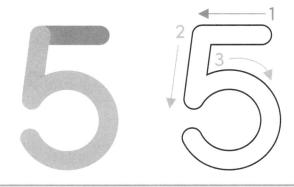

Trace the number. Start at 1 and follow the arrows.

5 5 5 5 5

5 5 5 5 5

5 5 5 5 5

How many beads are on the string?

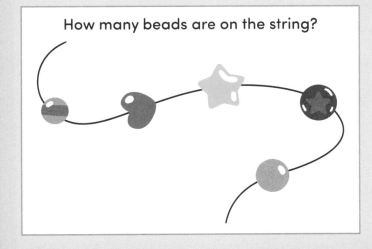

Use your finger to trace the number and say the number out loud.

six

Trace the number. Start at 1 and follow the arrow.

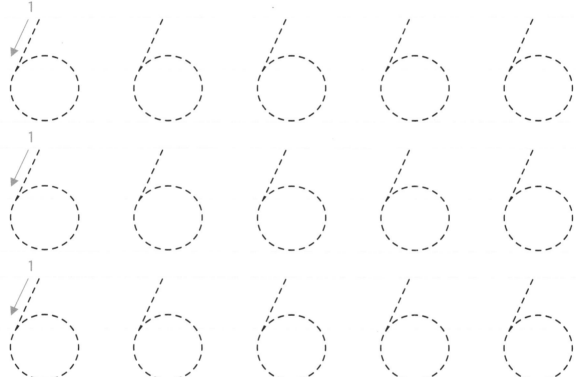

How many cookies are on the pan?

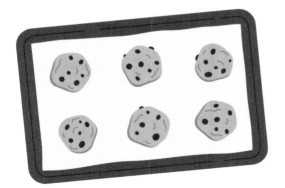

Use your finger to trace the number and say the number out loud.

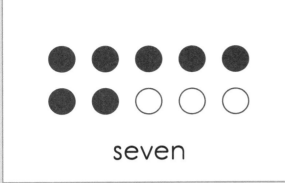

seven

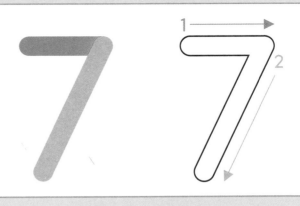

Trace the number. Start at 1 and follow the arrows.

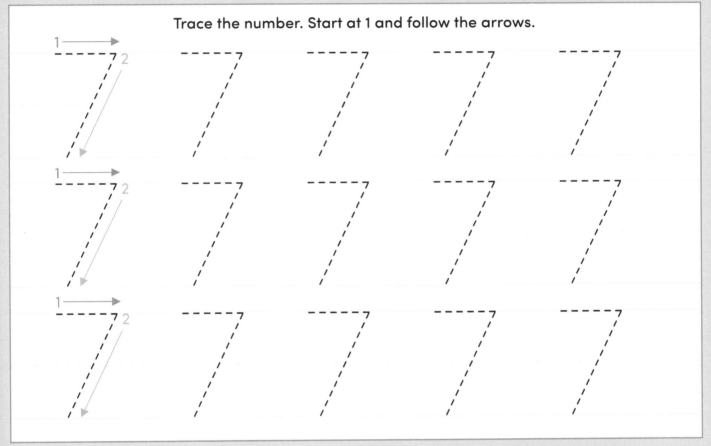

How many raindrops are falling?

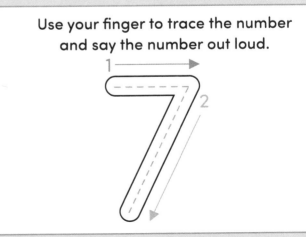

Use your finger to trace the number and say the number out loud.

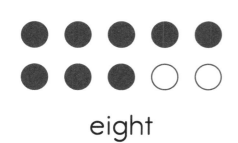

eight

Trace the number. Start at 1 and follow the arrow.

How many kernels are in the bag?

Use your finger to trace the number and say the number out loud.

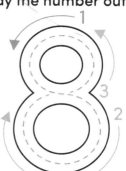

nine

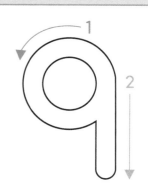

Trace the number. Start at 1 and follow the arrows.

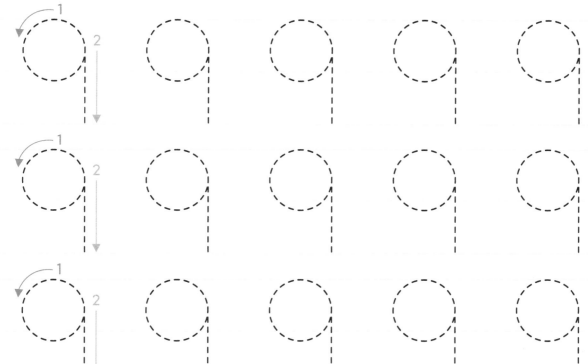

How many candles are on the cake?

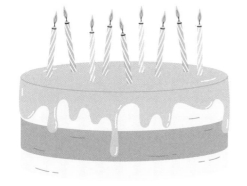

Use your finger to trace the number and say the number out loud.

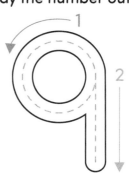

ten

Trace the number. Start at 1 and follow the arrows.

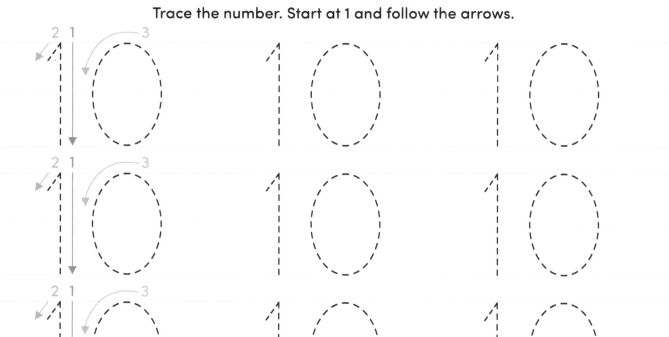

How many bubbles are in the air?

Use your finger to trace the number and say the number out loud.

Trace the letters.

Aa Bb Cc Dd

Ee Ff Gg Hh Ii

Jj Kk Ll Mm Nn

Oo Pp Qq Rr

Ss Tt Uu Vv

Ww Xx Yy Zz

Trace the numbers.

0 1 2 3 4 5

6 7 8 9 10

MY WRITING PROGRESS TRACKER

Color in the letters and numbers as you complete the pages.

Aa Bb Cc Dd
Ee Ff Gg Hh Ii
Jj Kk Ll Mm Nn
Oo Pp Qq Rr
Ss Tt Uu Vv
Ww Xx Yy Zz
1 2 3 4 5 6 7 8 9 10

WAY TO GO!

CERTIFICATE OF COMPLETION

has successfully completed *Big Handwriting Practice Workbook for Kids*

Signature

Date

About Applesauce Press
Book Publishers

Applesauce Press creates thoughtfully designed children's books that spark curiosity, creativity, and learning. With a focus on engaging formats and vibrant illustrations, our titles cover a wide range of subjects to educate and delight young readers. As an imprint of HarperCollins Focus, we are dedicated to bringing fresh, beautifully crafted books to families year-round. Learn more at cidermillpress.com.

"Where Good Books Are Ready for Press"
501 Nelson Place
Nashville, Tennessee 37214 USA